WISDOM *of* GOD

Enfold me

When the Angels reply

𝒜MELIA 𝒷ERT

Copyright © 2017 by Amelia Bert

TABLE OF CONTENTS

3

Preface

Many of us have questions about where we come from, about the world, about what is real; whatever we cannot grasp, we wonder. Wondering is indeed human curiosity to better ourselves. Now, what if all those questions we wonder about, could actually be trusted upon God? What if God replies?

"That would be awesome" I could imagine you say inwardly. Well, it is awesome, and it is even more awesome that you hold such impression right now! God has replied through Angels and lighted spiritual guides that lowered their vibration so that I, Amelia Bert, could hear their responses. And I did grasp them; I have collected them all, bound them together and I'm now making them available to you through this book. How awesome is that? Well, you can soon read the answers to your questions as they come directly from the Angels, directly from Source.

It is so ironic how we question so many things, even when the answers are within us all. As you read the responses from the Angels, you will realize that you know the answer already. Why is it so? Is it because we forget what we know before we embark upon each physical journey? Do we live forever? Here are those questions again, only a few out of a whole book that I have compiled.

I consider myself lucky to be able to connect with these lighted beings, to have the answers that so many of you wonder about. This is the sole reason why I decided to create this book, so that you will know the answers as they come from them directly.

If you don't know who I am, my name is Amelia Bert. I am a channeler, an intuitive, an Angel communicator. I "hear" Divine guidance as it comes through me. I translate the energy transmissions into words to understand what this source speaks to me. And then, I share what I know with all of you, because this sort of knowledge should be spread to everyone.

The energy and words of these lighted beings of God are full of love. I usually find myself in tears with the intensity of those pure emotions. Love is what God is, and Love is what is spread through Angels. This is how I am certain that what you are about to read is true guidance; this is how I know that what they speak is true.

As you read the answers to the questions that I have posed to them, you will realize that you know most of the answers already. This is because you are part of them, and they are part of you. You are Light, you are God, and so is everyone.

Introduction

"Dear Angels of the Light", this is how I began each question to receive guidance directly from the Light, through these Divine Angels that speak the word of God. And they always come forward to reply to the questions, always.

For this book, I don't take full credit; I recognize and appreciate all the help that the angels have given me to help me understand the words that they spoke. Archangel Gabriel was very close to me while I was typing this book, to make sure I didn't misinterpret any of the answers.

The questions are divided in two parts: Matter: Questions about the world and Essence: Questions about consciousness and spirituality. I welcome you in this path with answers to the questions that you have wondered about. As you find the answers, and as you understand them, you will become enlightened and more Divinely connected. Let the energy of their words move you to higher vibrations, to dimensions where love conquers all.

MATTER: *Questions about the world*

1.

*H*as everything been here forever, or did it begin to exist?

No, nothing had always been. Everything was first a thought, and then energy before it took a form. Same as you, same as us, same as the world in which you stand.

2.

How were humans created? How did we come to earth?

Similar to anything that exists around you, first it was a thought, energy, light, an idea. Like an empty canvas that begins to fill as you draw on it, that was all that the human form was. Then it was perfected, out of the knowledge of all the other animals that were created before it.

Every animal has its purpose; it will live to experience something new so that it offers an experience to the whole. For the fox it is cleverness and cunningness, something that an elephant is lacking. But the elephant experiences physical attributes of a big and strong body. So the human is created to be the smartest of all the others, to be able to feel and love, and equally create. To be able to expand unlike the other species.

And so, when the canvas was finished, and the image of humans was formed, God created "prototypes" and sent them on earth to create more. Similar to any other species that exist. Out of a few, there were more.

You did not simply appear on earth out of nothing, but you were formed with nature's supplies. The oxygen gives you life; it is to remind you of earth, that you cannot live without your mother. And so, earth was your womb. Like a flower that needs seeds to have life, you were formed out of human fetus that grew and existed in nature. How did a flower's seed form? It was created out of physical elements. How did any animal come to be? You were no different than all of these. First it was the earth that gave you life, oxygen and nutrition to form. And so, you were one with the other animals. You lived together, coexisted and learned from one another. You were a part of mother earth, cleverest yet with no remorse and consciousness. But God knew this creature's potential and wanted to experience it more, so He gave it consciousness to help it expand and grow. You were given a soul, and along with its power, judgment, emotion and remorse. Those emotions were dormant at first within, but they slowly

prevailed over animal instincts and this human animal was no longer like the others.

Whatever all the other animals had, humans had it even more be it curiosity, cunningness, cleverness, strength, love for one another, need for survival etc. And so, you slowly evolved based on all those animal instincts that existed and those human instincts and grew, and so you grew and you expanded. You become the human that you are now.

3.

What is the meaning and purpose of the universe?

Life is the purpose of the universe. In all extensions of time, in all the galaxies and realities, the purpose is for it to be a place where souls reside. No matter if those are physical or spirit, they exist within the universe to enrich existence as you know it. Without it, nothing would be possible, you wouldn't have knowledge.

4.

Will earth disappear? If yes, how will it happen and when?

Everything that is physical fades away. Earth too will follow this natural rhythm and dissolve.

This is not to happen for many centuries to come as earth has still an important part to play in all. As the place of learning, it shall continue to be so, for centuries equal to what has now passed.

You might sense the natural shifting and changing of the atmosphere of the earth. It is aging. As it does, new phenomenon will arise that will baffle many; things that humans have never witnessed before on earth, yet they are all to come as a natural way of growth of this living habitat. Yes, weather changes, lack of oxygen and overflow of the water bodies are few of such phenomena that it will experience as time goes by. However, as with anything else, earth also follows a natural rhythm. But like anyone who experiences angst and struggles, the strength fades faster. You, as a loving child of mother earth, should show appreciation, help, respect and love it, to give more stamina for earth to live longer.

Earth is not the only place of living for physical friends. Once earth fades there are more like earth, still young that shall continue their journeys of life lessons and experiences. It is not the end.

5.

How did dinosaurs get extinct? What was their purpose?

They came first, to form life. They came to test earth's habitat. Dinosaurs ceased to be because they have completed their mission on earth. Dinosaurs could not coexist alongside humans, they would harm and cause unnecessary struggle to humans. Their extinction was not random, but an evident outcome to their nature. The bigger dinosaurs ate the smaller ones you see, in the end there was none left.

The formation of dinosaurs exists in many animals today, even within you. They were the first species to leave their DNA in earth, and to all the other habitats. The way they have evolved, however, was unnatural for their existence. They could not provide for one another any longer.

As they have lived and formed, then other animals could not learn and exist. If the dinosaurs exist, they would not allow humans to thrive. They would feed from you; they will exceed you in strength. It would be unnatural and opposite of the nature of earth. You come here to learn, to create, to live and this is the way it should be. Dinosaur's path has ended before you existed and that was not random.

They came on earth to take form, to connect with nature, to survive on earth and give their imprint on other species. And they have done just that.

6.

Are there aliens? If yes, who are they?

If the concept of defining "aliens" is that: another form of life exists in physical form in other planets, then the answer is "yes".

Similar to the place you call "earth", there are many other various physical planets that may be similar, while others different from earth's qualities. Physical beings in those other planets experience life differently and have various qualities unlike your own. Some might be closer to your formation, while others are lacking, or are more advanced than human species. This is to show that life is experienced differently so that it brings new knowledge to the wholeness of the overall existence.

In those other planets and galaxies, life is formed differently but they too, are governed by free will and they have expansion to undergo and lessons to learn. They are not in fact different from your human nature, as they are directed, like you, guided upon and once they let go of the physical plane, they re-emerge, like you, into the non-physical to continue their mission.

In some planets, only different species of animals exist, that you have not seen before. This is because the formation of their planet has different qualities than earth and their way of life is unlike yours.

In planets that the physical beings have advanced intelligence, similar to your own, however, they have different formation and qualities. Some intelligent species live solely in water while others do not use language but connect like spirits, with mental communication. Some of these "aliens" are smarter, others have more physical attributes.

What might seem absurd to you is that many of you have actually lived in planets like these before. You were one of those species you call "aliens". This is because your soul wanted to advance differently so it chose another planet.

We don't want you to be afraid, or feel threatened as their existence does not threaten your own. Answer

this question for us if you must: "Are humans dangerous?"

The answer is yes and no, some harm others, some respond differently to something new than others. Some are violent, some are peaceful. So similar to all intelligent species there can be those who are very eager to learn, friendly and true, and others that advance based on force.

Have they ever visited our planet?

Yes. Some species are more advanced than you, but similar to you, they are curious about what else exists. They however have studied your human form thoroughly and they are now well aware of your potential. These species however are more advanced, they cannot be seen, so they can observe uninterrupted.

Not all species though are more advanced than you. There are others who are centuries behind in development.

What must be said nevertheless is that earth is a very difficult planet to live in. Many physical beings fail to follow their path and develop; there is a lot of misery and corruption that causes souls to advance more while on earth. But fortunately earth has expanded, and now all physical beings are moving towards "awakening" that brings them closer to their true potential.

Those who walk on earth are considered braver than others. However, earth is also so beautiful and so wise; it expands souls more than other planets' do. Those who focus on its beauty and learn to focus their attention to greatness, they succeed their path.

7.

What are the differences on living in other planets than living on earth?

Every planet is created in a unique way, to serve different goals. Many other living planets, that welcome physical incarnations, are created in such a way to offer various experiences to those living upon it.

For this reason, not one planet is the same as the other. Like all of you, you may have similarities yet you are different from one another.

The planets and physical dimensions that exist are actually plenty and we couldn't just give you all the information that exists in each one. But since you are curious we will mention a few.

In a planet called "Galanthia", it allows physical reincarnations like earth, but it also extends their living timespan. They have more time to learn and expand and gather many skills; triple as much time as you have now. This is because "Galanthia" offers many more opportunities, many more lessons than those on earth. The skills one can obtain have much to do with mental expansion and training of mental skills. The living friends on "Galanthia" called "Galathons" are not speaking a verbal language but rather their verbal speech is limited to sounds. They do not grow their food and they definitely do not cook it. What's more, In "Galanthia" they live based on emotions and actions. Their reason of being in that planet is to make better communication and deeper bonds with one another. For this they "feed" based on interactions, emotions and lessons.

Here on earth, you come to connect with mother earth, for this you grow your food to interact with it, to learn, to respect it. As you understand, you will see that each one has different qualities based on what attribute and skill one soul needs in order to expand.

Another planet with special attributes is planet "Eranus" this planet holds many of those souls that have inspired human imagination. There are animals that are very exceptional and unique, like your own unicorns. They learn to co-exist with one another in harmony; they have no power among each other. They in fact learn from each other so that each one respects the qualities that the other one has. This is a very peaceful planet.

A planet more similar to your own is called "Avsis". This planet welcomes physical reincarnations that are similar to humans. They do not need to breathe oxygen to survive, and they do not walk; they sway from one place to the other. They are only recently begun to form verbal communication to speak with one another. They are very clever beings, but they make mistakes, like you. They communicate based on their own understanding and for this their growth is not advanced. They rarely bond as a community but they respect one another. "Avsis's" mission is to provide physical beings space to grow and learn based on their own experiences and needs. They are not greedy or jealous because they do not care what their own does or owns.

We can go on describing different planets and their attributes but many you cannot understand them based solely on your human experiences. You have visited many other planets indeed, as you are free to choose once you return to the nonphysical.

What we have to mention is that you do not need to have a physical body to expand. There are many, many other planets that are a place for souls to visit and learn, and expand.

The cosmos is so big you will never be bored of it, no matter the years of your soul.

We love you unconditionally.

8.

Why do people suffer? Why do hunger,
diseases and hate exist?

They did not exist, they were created by fear. Fear is a negative emotion that welcomes more like it. If one spends too much time in one emotion, they become that emotion.

We speak for those that see darkness everywhere they turn, and they do not thrive with another's happiness but lust for it. Those, invite negative emotions and ultimately negative circumstances towards their path. This is when diseases spread, they were called forward. Similarly, any other negative event that takes place, it does so because of negative attention given to it. We did not say that you invite negativity voluntarily, but yet again energy knows no other but attention.

And so out of fear, darkness spreads, negative emotions bring misery along with other negative emotions that spread and cause unhappiness. You created those with your attention; they were invited in your life by no one other than you. Why don't you see that you are this powerful? You bring upon you all that you think, all that you believe and lust for; good and bad. Take responsibility of your power and work towards expanding yourself the way you want to.

And so, we told you how diseases spread, out of hate and fear. Now hate and fear coexist similarly just like the color black and white. They exist to bring variety, but they are there harmoniously, coexisting among others. Do you see white, or do you see black? Do you choose to add the color white in your life, color black or all in between? One exists just like the other, not to harm, but to bring variety, lessons, productivity. You turn where you choose to, no color calls for you, no emotion is more than the other.

And now we shall speak of hunger. "Those children that were born without much to live by, how could they have brought it upon themselves?" you ask us. They didn't, they chose to learn the value of having

little so they understand the gift of having more. As you embark upon a human life, you carry with you all the others as well. They might have been greedy, and laughed upon the other poor in a past life, so they chose to learn what there is to have so little. We are so very proud of those souls who know the value of learning and living by their mistakes so that they grow more aware, so that they advance. How can one come closer to God, closer to purification, if they do not understand some values? Values of humility, and struggle, modesty and kindness.as you know them you know more about power and abundance. And so if you have lived in both worlds you know more about the world, you earn more understanding, expansion, lessons and emotions. And then, the more you know— the more you progress, the greater, and purer.

So do not worry for our dearest friends because all have chosen their paths and those who walk upon having less than others, they are learning their lessons so they become stronger. Be proud of them as we are as well. Pity them not, but show them kindness, in the way that some might have shown you when you were on that path.

9.

Alternative dimensions, alternative universes, do they exist? How is it possible? Can I be in two places at once only in another time?

Can I have gone both left and right? Do both exist?

The world you see and live in, is a possible pathway to the plethora of options you have. Imagine a tree, what if you were small as an ant and you are at the trunk. As you walk up, you notice different branches, you make the decision to go towards a branch, as you do, you realize that this branch has other branches later on;

you make another decision as to where you will go next. The other decisions exist also however, but without you in them. You never get to experience what is like going on another branch. The one you have taken however has given you experiences and lessons and other choices to make. As you are incarnated on earth, you have so many choices to make every day, and you get to decide which way to go. This is your free will; life is the tree, and the branches your choices. If you did not select one branch, they still exist nonetheless. Do your choices exist as well? Yes, all the other branches are available to you, all the various pathways.

We, in the spirit world don't have to make these sorts of choices, because we already know which pathway they will lead us to. We already know the result. Before a soul incarnates, it knows as well, If not all possible pathways, most of them. All of you have inner guidance, if you trust your intuition, if you pause before you decide; it will direct you based on the awareness, based on the knowledge as to where will each pathway leads. If you ask us as well, we can guide you, but you have to know what you want to achieve from each pathway, what result will make you happy. Then if that is resonates with your plan, you will be guided to it.

Thus for your staring question, both left and right choices exist. While on a physical journey, you only get to make one. While on the spiritual journey, you already know the result and lessons of both.

We hope that we have cleared all doubts from our explanation.

Time only exists in the physical dimension you see, while in (the) spirit (realm yes you can be in two places at once, and even a hundred places. You already know what left is and where right will take you. While in a physical form; you are asked to make a choice so that you learn from the journey. Trust your intuition and have your highest good of all in mind before your grant selection of paths, then so it shall be.

10.

*W*hy do humans matter? *A*re animals as important?

Certainly, all species serve their purpose, and all of them came from one source energy, from what you call God. So why would you matter more than them? Is it because you have logic and they don't? Is it because you can rationalize and they can't? Is it because you can speak and they can't? Do not think of your human nature as more important because such assumption is not true. The fact that they lack some qualities it is not because they are not as important, but because they do not need them. Their purpose is different from yours. Similar to a bird that has wings and a bear that has fur.

Both of them don't need to have what the other does but they are both equally important.

As we have mentioned before, animals have a spirit. This spirit lives on, similar to your own. Their species exist to form life, to experience life, to learn, similar to you. A fish or a dolphin swims in the water, it does not need oxygen to breath, the experiences and journeys that those animals gain, are shared with source, so source can gain knowledge; so does a bird that flies free in the air. Also, this knowledge is shared with all of you, since you are part of the source of God. If you think about it, dream about it, you already know how a dolphin feels, you know a little bit about its experience. How is that? How can you know if you have never been one? This is because the dolphin's knowledge is source, and you are source.

11.

Why does time exist?

Time is there to keep order. How would you learn if you can do many things at once, be in many places at the same time? As time flows, it does so in such a manner, that allows you to focus and appreciate only a moment at a time. If all moments were happening now, you will feel disoriented, lost and miss many events that occur.

Imagine a world with no time. As you embark upon a physical journey, you live everything: life and death, childhood and education, mistakes and achievements. You wouldn't be able to focus, to learn, to heal if all those lessons happened at once. All events of your human experience will be at the now. So, to help you recognize, appreciate, have fun and relax while on a physical journey, time was created. It brings you peace, time to think, learn, focus and heal among other activities.

It is true, in other dimensions, such as the one we now are, time does not exist. This is because we have no lessons to learn, we already know what exists; what is, was and what will be. We do not choose paths as we are already familiar with their result. We can be in many places at once because we are omnipotent. Time does not exist in the non-physical, what you feel like years; to us it's just a second. This is the way we evolve, and that is the way you do. All that exists has a purpose, nothing is created randomly. Trust that all serves a higher purpose, all works for the greatest and highest good.

You are doing alright.

12.

Why do we have to sleep half of our lives?

Sleep has many purposes as well. First of all, it helps you to relax and calm your mind. If one overworks and gets no rest, they become sick. Sleep makes sure that you get a break every once in a while. As you do, you function better, your mind is clearer, your body is rested, and you enjoy physical life the most. Remember the last time you were tired. If your day has been full, at some point you do not enjoy it anymore. You feel stressed, dull and even sad. But as you wake up refreshed in the morning all of that is gone. Sleep serves that purpose, to make you feel relaxed, happy, and healthy.

Another important factor that sleep serves is inner connection. As your mind is silenced, resting; your higher connection is stronger. As you go about your day, full of thoughts, you do not allow this inner connection to take place. But alas, this connection is vital because it guides you. Your higher self knows what should take place, what lessons you need to learn, what paths are best for you, what ideas you need. As you rest your mind, your higher Self guides you, and you can listen through your subconscious. How many times have you got a great idea while you were about to drift to sleep, or through a dream? What about a solution that was clear to you once you awoke? This is not a random happenstance; your connection with your higher self is greater when you sleep. Sleep is a spiritual time as well.

And so sleep becomes a necessity to you, because without it, you can't function properly. If we let you decide when to sleep, most of you would rarely do, you will call it a waste of time, but alas you would be lacking all those mentioned before. So, sleep is very important and sacred for humans to live optimally both physically and spiritually.

13.

Will reincarnations ever stop? Why and When?

As you dwell in a physical life, you have the choice to either continue in another life, or remain in spirit form. Both are equally acceptable and both are your choices to make.

Dearest souls, reincarnations will never end, as there is always way of expansion and enlightenment. As you were born in this physical reality, you do so not just for personal expansion, but for universal one. Each soul contributes to a bigger picture, one that includes all of us together. Each thought you make is new, each one of you have a different way of thinking based on your different experiences and characteristics. And so, as these variety continues so are the lessons, and so are the reincarnations.

A soul chooses to end the cycle of reincarnations once they can no longer benefit from human reasoning. One soul can still choose to reincarnate, however, it might not be for its own benefit but to help others expand, heal, teach or assist. Many of the older souls still do this willingly to assist the younger souls. When we say old and younger souls, do not take this as a way of discrimination or as a way to distinguish between souls. In spirit, we are all equal, you see both older and younger. Souls have no ego and neither do they feel jealousy, but they are entwined in oneness and love. For this, all of us want to help others, inspire and assist in any we can.

So to continue to answer your starting question: "when will reincarnations end," if a soul acquires all in which it musts, if they learn from their mistakes, if they have accomplished their path, then they can rest in the non-physical. As one becomes wiser, they experience existing in more ways. They uncover more gifts, all of which bring closer to source, to creation. They understand more about existence, they feel even more freedom and peace. As one soul expands, they become

greater, more purified, more connected to source, to energy and to all that is. And from there, souls continue on completely different journey than the one of reincarnations. Reincarnating either on earth or in another planet, it is the beginning stages of learning and expanding. As one ends that cycle, they have more to go through; however the reincarnations are not needed any longer.

A soul progresses differently than another. One might take 1000 life of reincarnations to learn, while another might need 5000. Progression is based on lessons learned, pathways that are achieved or souls that are being helped.

14.

Is sex a sin?

It is surprising how such a small word contains so many contradicting vibrations and frequencies on its own. For some, sex means something beautiful, Divine even, while in others it brings so much disgust and sin.

Firstly, we encourage you to think about what it means for you. How come that some find it thrilling while others lustful? A word does not define your beliefs but what you make of them results in a word.

Whatever our response to you at this time, we do not wish to mark your own thoughts and beliefs on the subject. People believe what they want to believe, what their experiences lead them to believe.

A word on its own is not harmful or wrong. The act as God intended it; it is very pure and full of gifts to the human race. On the other hand, the way that some have misused this act, and how they brought pain and fear not only to some but to the entire world itself as you now ask us whether this act is a sin. The way that this act was misused made it a lustful and fearful act. It lost its pure divinity and Godly gift as it was is used with harshness, with power upon others. Those create fear, sadness and disgust with that act. Those who use this act without any pure or noble intention, then the act cease to be a Godly gift to mankind.

Anything that exists is not happenstance and is actually there for a reason. Your form is perfect exactly the way it is. Similarly, your needs are perfect and you do no need to be ashamed of them. As anything given to you actually serve a particular purpose and it is vital to your wholeness as a human being. The pleasure of taste, the pleasure of touch, the warmth, the emotions and the sounds you enjoy, are there for that purpose, and so is sexual pleasure. It is there to help you appreciate and enjoy life the most. Is it a sin to enjoy such pleasures? Is it a sin to enjoy sound, or appreciate taste of a food? Then why do you call pleasure of the body a sin, if it was given to you openly to enjoy?

Should you be shameful if you enjoy such pleasure that was given to you as part of your perfect nature? No. Sexual pleasure is a completion of the greatness that you are, of the gifts that were given to you so you could enjoy this physical life. So enjoy them openly with no discrimination and fear.

The same with anything that exists; if you become greedy, then will you lose control, you use the meaning of the pleasure, you do not appreciate it as much but you get lost in it. This is for all pleasures and not only this one, only then you should be wary of pleasures. Appreciate and enjoy them but do not obsess over it. Obsession, greediness and exercising power over someone's free will is what you should be wary of. Then you lose yourself, you lose your way, then only pleasure overshadows you.

So when you ask us is it a sin? We respond: it is what you make it to be.

15.

Is the desire for abundance of money and material things wrong?

How much should we have, and what should be the limits to achieve it?

Having the need for materials things is not a desire of the soul, but of the ego—of the character which masks your presence. That does not mean that it is wrong to desire, to lust, to want more because you wouldn't be able to desire anything. This desire is what makes you try to become better. It is one of the pleasures of being in a physical body, similar to taste and sexual pleasure. It is there to help you expand your horizons, widen your options and enrich your physical life.

54

Nonetheless, and same with all, having more of material things will not expand your spirit and neither will it help you to learn. It is only temporary so you should not spend your whole life trying and focusing on material things, or money. Instead focus on expanding your spirit, enrich your life with people, memories, give assistance and create ideas and organizations that will help others to do the same. Actions like this will stay, they will help you expand, and they will make you wiser.

16.

Why do females have to suffer to give birth?

Pain is part of the human experience. It is part of your human side. It does nonetheless result from the ego self and not from the soul self. The more aligned you are with your soul, the less pain you will subdue.

Souls, who incarnate, are aware of the physical form of pain and are willing to overcome it.

Giving birth and any other physical pain occurs to bring experiences. Change occurs to a female body, as the fetus becomes ready to be born, the mother experiences physical changes as well. It is the natural order of things. As change comes, it prepares for new experiences. Birth pain occurs as a release. It is the way of human structure, to be able to experience pleasures, pain and happiness. Birth is one great example of this.

Which one will you focus your attention on: fear of pain or joy of a new life? Choose where to turn your attention to. Most situations have the positive and the negative but it depends on how one sees it.

17.

What does it take to be healthy, and live a long and happy life?

This is an easy question for us. Embrace your spirit. Spirit brings you courage, joy, love, peace, power, healing. The more connected you are to your true self, the more your physical life and body welcome in those energies. You are surrounded by light and those negative human emotions become less evident within you. You will gain clarity, know your purpose; follow the inspiration and guidance from your inner self that will lead you to pleasurable people, events and circumstances. The more you allow the light within, the more it shines your life and body.

18.

Once I began the spiritual path, I felt alone. Friends I had left me, and I can't find people that match my vibration.

What do I do?

If you rely on others to be happy, then it means you do not love yourself enough. What we advise our physical friends who struggle to find acceptance and support from others, is that: you should work on your self-esteem. Others will love you only if you love yourself. As you do this, you will not seek for approval or support because you will already provide those. So now we ask from you: what do you want in a friend?

Give it some thought and once you visualize it speak it out loudly. Ask for those friends to show up for you, to stay and then watch what happens. Life is that easy you see, you should not see those who left and believe you were unworthy of them, let them go by knowing they were not vibrational match to your greatness. Once you are aware of this, then your energy will have shifted and you can attract friends of equal frequency to you.

You are not here to be alone. There are many others wanting to have a friend just like you.

19.

Is sex of the same gender wrong?

No. why would it be wrong if it is based on pure emotions of love and acceptance? If anything is based on those it cannot be wrong.

We do not approve of anything that is used to mistreat, to exert power, or that it is based on addiction.

Whenever two souls unite in this loving act, it is but God's gift to you.

20.

How should I live?

As you stand there, in your physical reality, you see and observe everything from a different perspective than the way we do. We see clearly what one must do to move forward freely, the actions to take to thrive. As we stand here, outside of your reality, or as you call it "outside of your shoes", the guidance that we will bring to you is rather vague. We do not have specific "rules" for you to apply, nor do we have the authority to tell you how to live your lives. Each one of you has a special pathway to walk and the way you do it, is what defines your success.

As we have mentioned earlier, all of you have different points of view. Some see life in a different perspective from others. The different characteristic of each one of you is what makes you special. The way you think, speak, observe and decide your next action is truly unique. What we do is step back, and let you live the way you chose. We let you make your decisions, live your own lives. Yes, there are times that you get confused and you feel lost. There are times that you are in doubt and hesitation. In those times, we cannot intervene to help you unless we are asked to do so. Even if we do come forward to help you find your way, we do it in a way that allows you understand your path needed, but find your own steps to get there. We can't tell you to go left; alas the right turn will take you there as well. It might take you longer, but both left and right will bring you different journeys. Who are we to decide that for you? Before you entered the physical life you did so by telling us "I make my own choices, I take my own journeys. If I need you, come and help me." And so we do, we look out for you from a distance, waiting for the time you will need our help, and then we do come forward to give you a "little push" forward not to tell you how or what to do. This is not our job, you see.

So, enough with all that; to answer your first question, our response is the following: You do what makes you feel good. Enjoy every moment of your physical life and trust that you will thrive in the end. Whatever

road you shall take, either that is left or right, you will get there. You might receive different lessons on the way, but this is why you are on earth, to live in a different way. So do that and live as you like, live happy, be free, and do not restrict yourself, your ideas or your urges. You have an inner guidance, a feeling that reveals to you what to do, what is right. Something like your own GPS systems. If you set it right, it will tell you right where to go next. So set your inner GPS and tell it where you want to go. It will take you there. Have a little more trust in you, and remember, if you ever need us, we are just a call away.

21.

What is DNA and what is the purpose of it?

What about your fingerprints? Aren't those different? What about your facial characteristics? What about your preferences? Your character? Why are they all different? Because you are never the same with someone else. You are special, unique in your own way and everything about you is as well.

Your DNA is only part of that uniqueness. It is there to define how different you are, the same with all the other differences that you have. DNA is but an imprint of your whole. An identity so to speak of who you are. It is there, as it also contains particles of your inner soul. As you combine with a body, so your soul merges with that body, for a deeper connection. The facial characteristics might be different from lifetime to

lifetime but the DNA is not. It stays the same, because your soul is the same. It is a unique way to define the essence of your soul. You are connected with all you do, with whoever you become. This connection is imprinted in your DNA. You are this person, and the one you were before is added on to become the wholeness that you are. Every lifetime makes you more perfect and unique. No one is like you in all the galaxies, and through all the lifetimes.

22.

How Does Memory Work?

Imagine a race. As you watch that race, you see the same runners doing the same thing over and over. As you watch 30 races with the same runners, do you remember all of the races, if all were the same? Someone escapes you, unless that someone is special, unless it has created deeper emotions within you. Then you will remember that one, because it was more unique for you. The same with your memory you don't remember all that occurs within your day because they were not associated with feeling. Those who were special, who got your attention you remember better than others, unless more of the same ones took place again and again. Then you differentiate among those "special" ones, and remember the most special.

Your memory is associated with your feelings. If you wish to remember something, add emotion to it. Then you won't remember with your mind, but with your soul, and that memory never fades.

23.

*I*s the bible valid? If not, please give a few examples where the meanings have been altered.

When one speaks a sentence, any sentence, and that one has been spoken to by 1000 people, will the meaning and essence of that sentence still remain pure? Will it be the same as it was first spoken to?

The bible is true; it is valid as it was firstly spoken, firstly written. As it changes hands, as it is re-spoken to many times since then, as it was translated and changed words from the original to another, from the new to the old, so it alters the words and thus the meaning is not the same. What we want to help you understand is that the words of God as they exist in the Bible or the testaments were pure but not anymore.

The words that were first spoken to those that God chose to speak them, were true and valid, however, those who have re-told it, re-wrote it so many times were not, and so the words changed and so did the purity, so did the truth.

So many years before when the bible was first created, the words meant different things. The way that those words were spoken, were meant to signify different meanings than those that are true today. And so, as years pass, so the words become more out-of-date. So those words lose their meaning.

What's more is that the words that were spoken by those chosen, meant different things than those who heard them, some of those meanings and examples and proverbs no longer stand to the world you know today.

And so, dearest ones, read the words that were spoken in the purest form possible, but as that cannot be, read with your heart and not thy mind. What do they mean to you? Be guided by your own divinity to understand them.

God chooses to speak to many people, and yes, even to you. Why do the words of God needed to be heard or known by those who spoke them so many years ago? Why not now? Why do you think that God only spoke to some so many thousand years ago, and is not speaking to you now? To all of you? Why do you think that only those words in the bible are the purest and that they only stand? Don't you think you are a child of

God as well? Don't you believe that you are special too? Can't you see that God wants to deliver you now as in the past? What has changed now? The messages are the same still, the love is the same, but you change, and so does the word to help you understand them better. Those new words are coming directly from you, from within.

They use to believe that only few spoke the words of God. That is not true, as God sees no-one as more special than the other, nor loves one more than the other. If you want to know the words of God, if you ask for them, then so God shall speak directly through you, the same as those words that found their way to you now.

It is alright dearest one, know the words then, but be open to the words now. They come from the same source and they are here to deliver you and to help you. Read them in their purest form possible but be wary so that they resonate with your truth.

You asked us for examples dearest. What are the bits and pieces that don't resonate with your truth from the bible?

Are those the proverbs and their meanings? Those were meant to give you examples of being humble, to remind you of what really matters. To help you remove the ego side of you and be more kind and pure to your inner truth. Is this the meaning that you understood from them? Or is it the words that were used to be

spoken? So, what if a word or even 50 words have been altered. What about the meaning of it all? Does it still resonate with your truth?

Some ask us about the evil. Jesus went to a place you call "hell" to rescue and suffice the dead souls that have fallen from grace. And so you took the word "hell" for granted and you believe that such a place exists. And then you made up of souls that go there unless they repent from all their sins.

Why do you think God has created "evil"? Why do you think such a choice even exists? Those acts that you call "sins", why did God create them if they are so unholy? It is not to test you, it is to let you choose, to fail and learn, to see the other side of everything. If you choose to do wrong acts, you grow some more, you recognize the value of being good, of being moral. It is not to test you. Even if one does not repent from their misdeeds, the lessons lie deep within their soul. Does it mean that they should go to "hell"? Why are you so fearful of such a place? Will God, the God of Love, want to cast you in an afterlife of pain and sadness? This is why you think He can cast you to such a place? If you hear your truth you will know that God wants you to be forgiven, to understand all your mistakes, before and after death and help you to repent, help you make things right, help you to return to light and love and not cast you in eternal darkness. And so, "hell" was created by the human mind, and every person that wrote the bible and re-told or re-wrote it, changed the meaning of that word into a real-like place that exists after death. We are here to tell you that no, such a place does not exist. God forgives, God loves. Even after death, lessons are still learned, choices are being made by you. You see the pain and wrong you might have caused to others so that you learn. If you did not understand, then God shall send you a lesson to help you understand. Those lessons are given to you by love and by the light of God to help you become better, wiser and more Divine.

And so, read the bible dearest ones but be wary as changes have been made to the words and to the meaning. And always remember that you can know the words of God, as spoken or shown to you directly by the Lighted source. Read and judge with your own heart.

24.

Can Animals Predict Earthquakes?

Indeed. Animals can see and sense shifts in energy. They have great instincts and trust their intuition. If their intuition alerts them to find shelter, they do. The same occurs with earthquakes and other events similar to it.

People can predict those as well. The more in tune with the energy that is around you, the more you sense shifts.

25.

Why does Gravity exist?

Gravity draws the energy of your physical body to the ground where it belongs. Without it, you wouldn't be able to "ground" to earth, to connect with your physical bodies in a way you do now. Also, you wouldn't be able to control the body of your physical energy. Gravity brings order, not only to you, but to all physical beings that walk on earth. Order is the best word we found to describe this. Time is another link you have that brings order.

Gravity, allows you to rely on your feet, it brings strength to your body because this way you can control it. Particles of air cannot control you as gravity takes a hold and dominates. In other words, gravity brings order. Order in regards to destination, to

posture, in the ability to link with earth. We really wouldn't have it any other way, and I'm sure you wouldn't either.

In other galaxies, it's true they don't go by the law of gravity. However their journey is different than yours. The beings that exist in those galaxies have different qualities, they don't need order, and they don't need a link with nature. You must understand that "earth" is a place that was created to bring value to those who walk upon it. To help them find link with nature, to enjoy their present (regarding to time), to be in order needed on earth so that chaos does not rise. Do not worry nor question about the others, as long as you are doing great where you are.

26.

Why do we dream?

As you sleep, your mind wanders. As you relax, your mind is only half asleep. It is in a trance state, but still awake. You might not realize it, but during sleep, some of your abilities are awake, while others are not. Your unconscious works, while you're conscious does not. While you still think, observe, you are not aware that you are doing so. You don't do it intentionally, because the consciousness is at rest. Similarly, memory does not work, since it is part of the conscious state, it does not "record" those experiences. The only way to remember your dreams is to recall your conscious state for even a split second. Perhaps a noise causes you to turn in your sleep, and in that split second you bring awareness, you get a glimpse of what you dream, or else, what you observe during your sleep.

77

Now, let's focus on where those dreams originate. As you don't have control while in your sleep, you are swaying from experiences that exist in your being. These might be thoughts that you had, images that you saw, feelings that you experienced. They are linked all together simply swaying from one to the other creating a pattern. You can't judge this pattern, since you are not conscious, you simply go along with it, and you experience it. This is only one part of what dreams are.

Another sort of dreaming, are the ones that are not created by you, but are brought to you by spirit. Indeed, the way we communicate is not through speech, but with experience. Similarly to the way you dream, one spirit brings you a lesson, a warning, healing through images associated with feeling. You call it dreams. They alter what you see and feel in order to help you process something that happened, help you understand or experience something, or even to let go of a blockage. Those spirits usually are your main spirit guides that "train" or "help" you while in sleep state. Dreaming works as a teaching method, or healing one.

27.

When there is life, is there a soul?

Living organisms exist to undergo a purpose. Not all living organisms exist with consciousness. They serve their own purpose; they live and grow until that purpose is fulfilled. If a consciousness or a soul will serve its purpose by being linked to such a living being, then they might choose to exist as that for a while.

What many don't understand is that even ants and tiny insects fulfill their own purpose. They don't need to have a soul to be respected. The reason behind their existence is enough to grant them worthy of being.

To respond to your opening question, not all organisms have a soul, however souls might choose to co-exist with living beings from time to time to observe, gain traits, and serve a purpose. For this, we ask that you respect all living beings as they are worthy of belonging, just the same way as you.

28.

What's at the bottom of the ocean?

If we keep digging and digging, will earth ever end?

Whatever exists does so for a purpose. Similarly, the sand and water are there to keep all the earth's people, plants and all that exists in the surface. The bottom of the ocean is there to keep balance, to hold everything together. For this, you won't be able to reach the end of the earth. Earth is there under God's command and so it shall never end. You can't reach the end because it will always be there. Without the bottom, earth will collapse and loose its balance. You can go deep within the earth, but not to the very end.

29.

What's at the bottom of a black hole?

Millions and trillions of little planets and stars. The black hole does not entail the end of the galaxy but a connection cord among others. Through the black holes you unravel another set of stellar and system of planets, some resembling your own.

Everything works perfectly as God intended. One matter completes the other so beautifully. There is no question about that

30.

Why can't the world be less corrupt?

Why is there night in the sky? Why isn't it always day? A very similar answer you will get from us. All exist to give different experiences, different outcomes, different people and different paths. If only one existed then it wouldn't be enough to create all these differences among people; the journeys and the characters. We are not saying that we enjoy a corrupted world, on the contrary. People make the world this way with the choices they make. None is born that way.

As you give way to the good in your heart then you learn to show mercy, love and appreciation. If however you were treated with disrespect, anger and hate then

you hold those at heart. World and people are created one way but they become another. The way you treat others it is the way you define yourself. If you seek more respect and kindness then show those to others and the world will gain more kind hearted people that fill the world with kind acts. Why should it be more corrupted than good? Why should you give way to the bad that exists? Give way to the good and you'll see that the more of that you will see.

31.

Why do newborn babies die?

The same as all who reincarnate on earth, these souls chose to come forward only for a while in this physical world. These souls might have some unfinished business, some lessons that they came here to learn very rapidly as their way for expanding. Their brief time here on earth might be limited but is not going in vain. They chose a brief lifetime to speed up their lessons.

Another reason that babies might die so early is to teach their parents life lessons. Loss is still a lesson needed to acquire for one to learn to treasure life. These souls agree to come forward and they pause

from their own expansion to help a family learn from their loss.

How can one learn to celebrate life if there is no loss? It is true, you never really die, rather you keep ascending. In order to ascend you must learn lessons needed of both life and death, of love and of loneliness. As both exist, both have their values and reasons of being. God never makes a mistake.

32.

Is it okay to eat meat? What should we eat really?

Your body needs energy to empower. This energy comes in the form of food you consume. As anything that exists has energy, the food has as well. Energy is transmitted by others around it, those who handle the food before you eat it, those who grow the food. This is equally true for animals themselves.

A potato for instance gains energy from earth, thus its energy is purer. A farmer might have put the seed, but it is earth that grew it with its energy and care. The farmer again picks up the potato from the ground when its ready, but the amount of time he spends handling the potato is too little to pass on great energy

to it. Thus the potato remains pure from the energy of the earth.

Now let's take the example of meat. A cow is a big animal, most of you eat it. The energy that a cow has is much greater than the one of a fish. It gains more energy from the surroundings you see, in order to sustain itself. For the cow to grow up and become ready to be consumed, it goes through different stages depending on where it is. If it is a farm, it runs around in the field it is closer to nature, it is treated with love, then that animal will be happy thus the energy purer. On the contrary to big sheds, where cows spent most of their time being captive, dirty and usually hungry. You see, the energy of the cows will be different as to how they have lived. At the end of their lives, when they are slaughtered, they suffer pain. That pain stays in their energy and thus in the meat you consume.

And so, when you ask us "is it okay to eat meat", we won't tell you it is not right to eat meat or that it is morally wrong, since animals feed on animals by nature. But we do tell you that anything that you consume has its own energy and when you consume it, it attaches to you.

If you pray for the food before you eat it, you give time to bless it and purify its energy.

33.

Why are there so many natural disasters?

They are the "aftermath". They occur as a result of negative attention, neglect and hate. All the negative attention becomes absorbed by nature which alters its natural flow.

Earth does not want to punish you, God is not vengeful, but attention returns back multiplied and unfortunately sometimes with negative results.

If you showed more care to earth than hate, if you were more grateful of what it brings, then earth will reward you, the same way it does many years since the beginning. But if you create nuclear wastes and fumes, and trash ~~so~~ then earth brings forth tornados, floods and earthquakes.

Again we must explain that those are not punishment from anyone, but a result of your actions. As you give attention, you get that attention in equal measure.

34.

Why does the sun go on shining?

Why does the sea rush to shore?

Why do we need oxygen?

Nature is created in that way to serve a purpose. The sun brings warmth, light and energy. Without the sun you would have been cold, dark and drained. It shines because you continue living and it will be for as long as you need it.

The ocean travels, the waves help you move from one place to the other while on a boat. With movement the ocean keeps the waters clean so you can find food. The

waves move you towards the shore so if you are ever lost you will find your way. The waves also help the fish travel.

The oxygen that you breathe rejuvenates you, helps your brain function clearly. You receive energy from the environment, in this way you are connected with earth, and linked with its own energy, the same way gravity holds you down. Without gravity you would be free to travel, earth will not be your home; you will be like a soul. You will be disoriented, lost and you couldn't complete your purpose while on earth.

35.

Was the bible really channeled by God?

In earlier times, people were more connected with own divinity. There was not as much hate and ego in one, so the people used to find peace and soothe when going deep inside themselves, when they were in quiet and solitude. As more of them did so, the thoughts became clearer; they could listen to their inner voice with more clarity. Yes, the bible is channeled by God, by a higher power that is connected to all, the same this book is bringing forth now. This is the inner peace and quiet that is needed to connect with your higher voice. As you do, you can find direct guidance not only for universal matters, but also for personal ones, to find your inner peace and life path.

And so, back to the Bible, it is true but many things are altered. So many years worth of leaders and pastors that were not so connected to their own divinity, found some of the words to be absorbed, cruel. Some laughed at them and crossed them out. The bible you read today is not intact the way it was written, the way it was supposed to be. But yet you hold onto it so strongly, you worship its words and you refuse to replace them with any other. You already know the truth in the words; you have your inner voice, your inner guidance, your own connection to God. If you trust another blindly, you will be misguided. Since then there were many words spoken by many, many books written that might not be called bibles but they are true. This is one of them, but it is not the only one. And we tell you, you don't need books to find the truth. You can channel it also. The way this author writes this book; because none is more special than the other.

Do not focus on the words of bible blindly. It has truth in them. It was channeled by God, by angels, by universal truth, with the help of those kind people that could listen to the voice within. We thank them dearly for helping others know these words, they have done well. But since then the words have changed, others have been muted, deleted, some have been altered.

Believe what you know is true. Trust your own inner voice more than others.

36.

Why didn't you prevent world wars?

Indeed, bad exists so we could appreciate goodness. Wars occurred because of a choice of some that led the others. We could not intervene with free will. But yet again lessons occurred from such events, that made bonds, and for people to appreciate and vouch for world peace. To know that such a thing is vital for not just the inner and outer peace of the world but also for individuals in it. As this world undergoes, and still does such bad events, you learn, you appreciate, you value.

So many lives ended tragically, so many dear souls were traumatized and we couldn't save all but we did

save a few, even if those stories are untold, we did do our best to prevent losses. Because those world wars hurt us as well, we did not like to see so much tragedy, hate, so many souls wrecked and even now some still recover and will do for years to come. Such a thing that happened is tragic and we did not approve, but yet we could not prevent, we could not intervene. What occurred now is passed, looking back to that will not help you to move forward, all you can do is to make amends with the events, with the choices of those few. They did learn as well, those who made those choices learned and deal with the pain they have caused.

But all that there is to do is notice the outcome the good that came from all that. It brought some together; it taught you that war is not the way. Those who listened now know. Such a big war is now in the past. It will not happen again as people are now coming more together. All of you prioritize happiness and peace; those new leaders that are to arise will not work with such cruel leadership. A new era has arisen out of the past one, and this is why the old one needed to occur.

37.

What are the cures for the world's biggest health problems, like cancer, heart disease and dementia?

With faith, as long as they believe that they will be healed, as long as they ask for God's help, as long as they remove any darkness from their life, so God responds. God listens and helps those who ask for help.

If such diseases come with no intention of staying, then they will not stay for long but only pass you by. If those however, come to teach, to help you grow, expand. Then those might stay longer until you learned some of the values needed. Some lessons are harder to acquire than others. Part of these lessons souls choose will reincarnate into one human life to learn so that they expand in spirit after their passing. Some of those lessons might not be understood while in human form

but they make sense as you return to spirit. Some of these diseases might come to "rescue" you from pain from this lifetime.

Others come as a warning to revalue the choices that you have made, to be a red flag for the person that you have become. They bring you a big alert to revalue, to make different choices, to return back to God.

In some other times, those big diseases come to bring lessons to others. Not many times children who suffer from those or something untreatable come to bring a lesson to the parents. You might say it is a cruel lesson, why does God allow this to be in such a way. Alas, some of the lessons are harder to be learned than others, worth lifetimes of life lessons and choices. Those forms of lessons don't act as punishment but as an extreme measure to return you back to a mission that you have detoured from.

Pray to God and have faith. It shall be resolved, as God works with your best interest at heart.

38.

How do we deal with anxiety?

Why do you worry and fear, dearest child of God? His love for you is great and the assistance He brings you is present whenever you call. Why do you worry and fear? To help you deal with this, you have to find the source of your angst. What matters cause you discomfort and furthering from love and light? As you identify those, pray to Lighted angels to carry those away from you, to help you remove their negative doings from your life and thoughts.

Whatever is causing you to lose focus and make you struggle, are sources that need to welcome the light of God. To shine the light upon those areas or topics is to help you illuminate that part of you that is scared. As you welcome positive emotions for what you fear and

worry, then those negative emotions will be replaced. Here is what we mean. If one worries for lack of money, find a way to soothe that worry so it doesn't bother you anymore. Why do you fear for money? Is it because God wants you to suffer? When you pray and ask for what you need, then God hears your prayers and responds. So why do you worry now if you have prayed for what you need? As you relax and allow God to guide you to a solution, then there is no reason for you to worry. Give these fears to God and He will lead you to a positive outcome. It is alright if you wait a bit more for this outcome to arise because you are well right now. You have all you need at this moment; you mustn't worry for the future, but exist in the now. And right now, in this moment, you have all you need. There is no need to worry. For later, God shall provide. So release your worries and fears to God and His angels and trust that the light within this topic will suffice and resolve it soon.

And so, have we succeeded to ease your worry child of God? What else bothers you? Pray for that to God and ask that He sends you a solution and a path that is evident for you to follow so that you find the solution. Remember that right now, it is okay, you don't need to worry all is well and God hears your prayers.

Talk to God, talk to His angels, so that they can carry the fear and anxieties away, so that they help you find solution and a well-given outcome to what bothers you. This is how you cease the worries.

39.

Does the loch ness monster exist?

Such a monster as you call it has never walked on earth. However, many other species have existed. This one was actually created to deceive.

40.

*W*hy should I be mortal at all?

But you are not. You are eternal; you have always been and always will be. What is not eternal is your body. That body fades, not to slow you down, but to give you choices and more opportunities to start again.

As you stand in the physical, you might dislike that you will have to give the body and start again. You think you will lose of all that you are, of all that you know. That is not true. On the contrary, all that you are will only be richer and wiser. All that you know will join you once again.

Think of a life that is miserable. If the choices made were of poor judgment, if the lessons that needed to be taught were not so bright. Then you would have that one life to live like eternally. You wouldn't be able to be someone new, to make other choices, to meet new people. If one was the same forever, then there will be nothing knew learned. They will be trapped in their choices forever, not expanding. The change is a transformation not of loss, but one of elevation and advancement.

So In other words, you are not mortal, but your body is. But this is not to keep you grounded but to allow you to fly and be better, bigger and wiser.

ESSENCE: *Questions about consciousness*

41.

What happens when we die from this physical life?

You can never die; you only evolve and change in shape and form. Your physical body may undergo changes, but we care for your soul that will continue the travels without the physical body.

As soon as the body stops being, your guides and angels that looked over you while in each physical journey will call for you. They send you assistance in order to find your way from the physical dimension to the non-physical one. Some might experience bright light; others might hear a song calling them to the appropriate direction. Each time however, they are filled with Divine peace and a knowing that all is well. Fear does not exist in spirit so you see.

When the soul is ready to move from the physical world, they follow their guides' call and they "leap" into the spiritual level, where all souls gather to coexist. This level is not physical and it cannot be described with human symbols. This is a state of pure joy, contemplation, acknowledgment and fun. Each spirit is free to observe, interact, learn and expand the way they please.

Usually when a physical journey comes to an end, the soul is greeted by all their loved ones in a union of love and peace. They are reminded that what once was lost can never be lost in the real sense of it. They are reminded of their spiritual essence in order to let go of fear and any human emotions that might overshadow them. Once they are ready to move on, they contemplate upon the life they have experienced. That life's journeys become imprinted in their wisdom and the lessons they have learned give them more power, more self-control. If a dear soul is too overwhelmed by the human pain, suffering or if their life has been too troubling, they undergo an immediate relief from that suffering, they are moved into another spiritual plane to restore their energy. Once they are strong enough, they can choose to reincarnate once again. They might choose to interact with other dear souls in love and harmony, they might even choose to observe another's life, or assist another which is in the physical.

You must understand that in the spiritual plane, there are no human emotions such as grief, blame or anger. The only emotions that exist are bliss, peace, harmony and love. For those of you that might believe of heaven or hell, we tell you that there is not such a place, as that was only creation of the human mind. All souls are greeted equally, no matter their journeys. If they have made good choices, they grow, they become enriched with gifts and talents, if they made poor judgment, in their next new life they must learn of the suffering they have caused, in order to learn and continue to evolve.

As you see, there is no punishment here, only lessons.

If you are wondering if you will see your loved ones once you join spirit, the answer is yes. They will be there for you, all of them not just those who were gone, but you shall see them all as there is no time in spiritual planes. You might not see their physical bodies but you will know it's them, you will know. Knowing is how nonphysical beings communicate.

You should not fear of death as that can never be. It is only a new beginning, contemplation and fun, because it really is fun to be in spirit.

We love you unconditionally

42.

What about the devil? Can we receive harm from dark spirits? How can we protect ourselves?

There is not such a thing as the Devil. It was created by human imagination to mask darkness. Human mind could not comprehend how a creator that is so kind and powerful and good would bring forthcomings, misery and fear upon people. So they hid all such dark matters in one and called it Devil. They go on believing that nothing bad can come from the source that created such good and gave life. What you must understand is that all that life brings does come with lessons, gifts and expansion, no matter if they are good or bad. Some souls wish to experience sickness so they choose this life to walk upon when on earth, not to bring misery but to inspire others, to gain strength and experience that side of life, so that they understand and appreciate another life more.

How can you understand pain if you have not lived it even once? Then you could not comprehend how important health is. You cannot value happiness if sadness does not exist. You see one source has everything, good experiences and bad, and it is you who can focus on which one. Do you see only misery, or do you experience the joy?

And so, back to your standing question, the devil does not exist; it was created to mask darkness and all those negative emotions.

Many spirits exist, and the same as human characteristics; they have good attributes as well as bad ones. There is not to say which one will prevail at what time. It saddens us that some souls experience so much pain in a physical life that carry it on once they pass. Then their human emotions mend with the spiritual ones. Dark souls as you call them carry the pain and darkness of a recently lost soul and can pass it one to the surroundings similar to a spirit who communicates with no words.

Souls are not naturally dark, or evil, or sad. The natural state and path of a soul is that of peace and love and happiness. Only on rare occasions that the soul becomes stubborn or confused to re-experience such emotions and keeps carrying on the way that it's recent life did. This is not to say that such souls are not being helped. You have help anywhere you are, and guidance but you also have free will. If they continue to persist, they hang on stubbornly to what they once knew; unwilling to move on and expand. Then these are the souls you know as ghosts.

They are confused and lonely, they hardly ever harm. They scare yes; some willingly while some are not. After time they understand that it is in vain and they move on to continue their journey.

If a soul causes harm, it does so rarely. We do not wish to frighten you at all. We feel uncomfortable discussing such souls because they are very tenacious and sadden us. There are such cases, but again as is free will, no one can impose doings on anyone in spirit world and so they run free to be as they wish. They may harm physical bodies temporarily, drain energy from where they can so they can sustain their own. You see energy comes from source, from positive emotions and so does healing. Once the soul denies those, it stays hidden, but it still needs such energy to sustain. So they "steal" from those who have and are vulnerable. Humans are connected to their divinity and while in a physical body constantly gain energy from their Higher Self. But once the body fades, the soul must re-unite with their "higher" self, their wholeness back to purity and love and joy. If such a soul refuses to return they will need to be sustained elsewhere. Again as this is not the natural journey of this soul, it is uncommon for one to stay longer than usual. Usually, those who do stay, they are fearful of judgment for that life they had, fearful of repaying the pain they caused.

Here is what defines ghosts from "dark souls" as you call them. The primary is confused, lost or afraid. Usually they do not harm but take their time reminiscing about the past life. The latter ones are masked by guilt and human emotions of ego that masks their purity and by choice they stay in the physical dimension, never experiencing the return to their own Divinity.

Humans can easily stop on both by choice. Most souls understand free will and respect it. They will leave you alone if asked. The others can be taken back if they choose to and many of us take this task to assist them in crossing over. To souls that are "dark" by choice they don't usually return, but they are fearful of the light and any lighted beings that exist because they

know they have more power over them. So once you ask any angel for assistance, they will guard your light so that no soul can harm it.

We want to set your mind at ease, reminding you such dark souls are few and do not lurk when light exists. The more happy, peaceful and connected to your divinity you are, the more those dark souls fear you.

We love you and we are by your side as guards of Light.

43.

What is deja-vu?

As you go about your day, you notice moments that feel like they have been lived before. You experience them with all your senses, even the thoughts feel the same but they are only a few seconds and then this feeling is gone.

These moments may seem as unimportant to you at that time, there are usually simple every day events, yet the sensation and feeling you gain from them appears as if they have been played before.

Have they? You ask us. The answer is No. they haven't, what you are experiencing in the life in which you live, it is lived once by you. Life is not a loop that keeps repeating as some might think. You are experiencing these moments with all your senses just one time and then the next moment is different. Not to be repeated again. Thoughts change, same as settings, people and concept. So it is unlikely that even for a second you will leave something twice the same way.

What you are experiencing is not reliving of a moment, but rather living a new moment in which you have sensed before. Not in a human living experience, but while in spirit. What we mean is, while in the non-physical, you can re-live one occasion several times the same way, as if in that physical body. There you observe, you capture, you understand, you notice. The moments you feel you re-live are non-other than moments in time in which you have visited before reincarnation. As a spirit, you cannot alter a moment you have lived or will live, you only observe. Similarly to your "déjà vu's", you cannot alter such a moment. Any change you might try to make has already been done by you. For this, déjà-vu is such a moment of observation. That second, your higher self or soul, takes over your living experience to observe and live through the physical body. When you sense you are living a moment, it is because you are, your soul is anyway. But it is only a moment and it is gone, there is no need for the soul to stay longer, one small second is enough.

44.

Are we being guided to what we are supposed to do? If yes how? What is a life's path and how do we find it?

You have an inner knowing about what to do, about what you are meant to follow while in a physical journey. Not every one's path is the same and not all will find it. You see, there is an inner knowing but if your mind is full of doubt, feelings of low self-worth and fear you do not receive the messages and inner guidance from your higher self. When time is right for you to complete this path, we assist you. Your dearest guides will send you signs and people to pull you towards the right direction. Then you have a choice, to follow it or not. But the signs and Divine directions are going to be appearing repeatedly to help you awake your inner knowing, until you become aware of them.

A life's path is not always a profession, or a business. It can be to inspire others, to be a leader for others or even a guardian of one person. Whatever that path is, it is chosen by you before reincarnation as something valuable that will help you as well as others to expand and grow.

Some incarnate willingly with more than one path to follow. When you follow your inner knowing and get to what you are supposed to do, you know it. You have inner confirmation, emotion of self-worth, pride, joy and a feeling of accomplishment.

Again do not be discouraged if you haven't found it just yet. It doesn't mean that you should quit your job to get to it. All you have to do is be more aware and open to the universe's guidance. Synchronicities are not random; on the contrary they take you to where you are supposed to go.

Just ask if you are ready to find out, and then listen, be aware, be conscious and alert. We shall guide you.

45.

Who decides when we die? Is our death predestined? Is anything else already predestined?

The journeys that you make while in a physical experience are not predestined. You have to learn lessons so you expand and gain wisdom so you can continue to expand greatly while in non-physical. For this, many pathways open up for you to give you those opportunities to learn and expand. Nonetheless, you can miss them or chose to alter those missions and follow another pathway. Whatever you chose, your soul learns. But as for mistakes, when you keep repeating the same ones you cannot learn nor grow.

The same is with a path; those missions are there filled with what your soul needs in order to grow.

The way someone dies most times is not predestined. The same is with the time of death. Usually your guardian angel protects you from death if you have still room to learn and grow and expand while in one lifetime.

Sometimes, another's bad choices may work against your own and cause you to end your journey prematurely. Those souls have to learn for what they have done while in non-physical. This is just to give you an example that even though there are some pathways and options for how anything will be, but it can ultimately take another way. There is nothing final, even death, because there is free will.

46.

Who is God? How did God come to be?

God is essence, God is purity and God is light. What you see, what you exist in, was created by God and it is not God. The energy that exists all around has part of God that connects all beings and species to one another, as well as with the one energy of the creator.

God does not exist in words you see nor actions. God does not belong to any category that can successfully identify his essence. God is harmony and power, God is creation as well as existence. Trying to identify that which he is, cannot be described in words.

The best way to help you understand this essence that is God, is to connect every wonderful emotion you ever had and magnify its intensity. This is how God feels; total purity, joy, Divine love and ultimate peace and harmony. None of these emotions can be felt by one without knowing the power that is God.

You are all connected to this power of God that exists within you.

God is creation. Before that none existed. God was peace and harmony that begun creating worlds to share His gifts. Then worlds were formed. God created existence as you know it now, to share thy gifts of "heaven".

As God is purity and inner peace, so God formed you and gave you reason and choices to feel the power that is God, to feel the power that exists within you. Come child of God; search deep within to find this power, to find this connection with the creator, to become one with all.

Instead of asking us to explain to you who God is, we encourage you to feel God within. He comes forward to those who want to meet Him. Find the power of God within you; notice its glory and purity. God is with you now.

47.

*W*hat can an angel do? *W*hat are their powers and limitations? *W*ere angels once humans?

We, Angels are a set of spirit souls that have no physical body. We wish to bring harmony among all that is, and stand as supporters to the goodness that exists and the power within all.

Usually, we have not been reincarnated as humans because their path is not to learn and experience like you do. We gain their wisdom and lessons by helping others.

We too can expand and learn and gain new traits and strengths. Like humans and any other being, we too have different characters and knowledge among each other. Some of us might focus on helping people expand; others might assist those who lost their way, while others prevail in time of crisis. Some can heal better than others, some can direct, others stand as guardian angels to soul while there are those Angels who oversee creations.

Because we have not been in a human body, we do not have egos. We are very pure, true and full of unconditional love for all.

You have asked us how Angels help humans. What are our strengths and limitations? We chose various ways to communicate, some direct and advise through dreams, others with synchronicities, others connect with people close to you to help you. Sometimes we might take higher risks to prevent a crisis. There are instances that we have spoken to one to warn them. We can grasp ones' attention with flash of light, a thought that keeps repeating, and a form that disappears.

All spirits respect your free will. We will not save one that does not want to be saved. We cannot help someone that has never asked for help, that it has never prayed. With your free will you allow us, angels, to take over and assist you. Our limitation lies in your responses and free will.

48.

What is the story of Christ? Why did He suffer in that way? What is the lesson behind His life?

People at that time, needed a direction. Those who lived then, or those before, were very confused. They knew no sense of God. For this they were lost, didn't believe that there is savior for them.

With no faith people were miserable. They did not pray because they didn't think anyone was there for them. They felt alone physically and spiritually. For this they stopped trying to be better, to be good. Depression was of very high radius and suicides where very frequent.

127

Christ came to show direction and give hope to those who needed it. With the teachings of a merciful God, of oneness and unity, people grasped on to faith and treasured it to help them through difficult times. Suicides and depression became less indeed, and the people found their sense of purpose.

Christ may not have touched all with His teachings, but His life has helped many, and even today His path brings hope and unity. His death was not in vain, He came forward willingly to help all of you and He would do it again. His suffering was a price He paid to make His teachings greater. He fought pain, he fought despair, he fought judgment, he surpassed all those fears and emotions not because he was special than any other, but to show you that you can too.

49.

Do animals have souls? Do they reincarnate?

Did we or will we live as animals?

Wouldn't it be unfair for you to live after death and for them not to?

What makes you so special and them unfortunate?

Animals do live on, the same as you, and use their physical incarnations to learn and expand, just as you. They too choose their next place of incarnation even if that is on earth or in another planet.

What makes animals different from you is not the same way of life on earth or after it; it is just their own way of dealing with their experiences, of relying on their animalistic instincts to survive. Animals don't reason like you, but still they form life, they strive to survive, and they learn how to be greater. Their difference is

129

relying on their instincts and bodies, and becoming one with nature. They too have a purpose and a soul.

It is different from yours indeed. Souls who incarnate as humans do not choose to transform as animals. They carry on the physical reincarnations with more intellect. Animals choose to be so and gain attributes based on different species.

Animals have purposes as well, they come willingly to join a physical life to either contribute to the whole circle of life by being a small fish, or a chicken that gets eaten, or to be a loving companion and a friend to a child, like a dog or a cat, or expand their own experiences by being a lion, or a dolphin. In any way they choose to come forward, those souls live on in the nonphysical, like you and they learn from their incarnations.

A form does not need a soul to be alive. It can sustain itself from energy. A human body can live without the soul, but it would be empty. With that in mind, know that souls do not give life, but they fill it. Not all forms of life have souls.

Souls choose to join a life if there are attributes they can benefit from. For this all humans have souls, but not all living organisms. Not all insects carry with a soul, unless a soul chooses to join them. There is a lot to benefit from all forms of life, and souls know this.

Respect animals and all life equally.

50.

If reincarnation exists, how do we choose our next life?

Reincarnation does exist. You are learning and expanding with every life you live in any body that you are. Everyone has gone through different journeys, different lifetimes and different decisions for this, their expansion varies. One might have the skill of playing the piano, but another might have the skill of playing the guitar. This is what makes each and every one of you different but so very special. Based on all those various experiences and lives, you experience life in different ways. Your capabilities and lessons are imprinted into your subconscious and help you make certain choices, even if you are consciously unaware of it.

And so, as all those lives actually exist within you, each new incarnation is chosen carefully by you, and by your guides, to help you cope with certain experiences, and gain skills to thrive in later incarnations. Each one of those lives completes your wholeness, like a piece of the puzzle that without it, you would be lost, incomplete. Even if one lifetime has caused you suffering, stress or unhappiness it taught you lessons, values and skills to make you stronger and wiser for the next one.

You have "missions" or else certain believes and desires that you want to accomplish that have to do with helping, providing and/or guiding others and the world. Either that is being a teacher to others, or an inspiration to help some achieve their own paths, whether that is assisting the world to be stronger in the form of a great leader, or an environmentalist who helps earth; or Your life's path might be inventing a gadget that will make life easier. Anything that this life's path may be, it has to do with the bigger picture, something bigger than yourself, and each lifetime helps you complete it; if not all at once then bit by bit.

Take for example the life of Christ, He did come forward, his reincarnation mattered so, and He completed it. Now there is no Need for more incarnations as he succeeded, he helped others, He expanded. Now he is helping from the non-physical, He is closer to Divinity and Purity than ever before. The same is with you, once you learn, once you complete your life's path, there will be no need for any more reincarnations, and you will help others achieve their path, guide and exist while being more powerful in spirit.

And so, to answer you first question, your incarnations matter and they are not chosen randomly but with care based on all the things you want to learn, all the people you will help, based on the greater impact your life will have. You do matter to us, you do matter many, and you are becoming greater and greater.

51.

How are souls created?

Souls are not born into existence, they are not formed either. Souls are created the same way God was. This is because all souls together form God. Souls exist, much like stars that shine. Souls are forms of energy. How does energy exist? It exists all around but not all of it is active you see. If all energy was active at once then there would be so much strength all around that it wouldn't be able to cope itself. This "Energy" exists all around, it is slowly coming together when time is right, to bring about new life. Life exists in the form of emotions, existence that is abstract. Once it begins to interact, it observes, it begins to create. As it begins to create, it begins to learn, experience and then it expands.

135

This is why you are one with all, because you come from energy that is all around, you see. You are energy, but you can create more energy, you can expand and grow and experience. You are part of God which is the same.

The time a soul is generated and takes a form has various stages. All that exists, the form of God that you know is LIGHT. As this light generates thought, or desire, it forms several particles that eventually "split" from the wholeness of that light, and stand alone. This piece of the light goes on to become a stand-alone soul that is still connected to the wholeness of the light, yet it forms different characteristics. Several of their characteristics are stronger than others, as no soul is same with another. This is particularly so, to exist and provide different results for the existence of the whole.

As this soul or part of light grows, it generates more light. With every choice, every lesson it grows and becomes stronger. The purpose of the soul is existence and learning and being. Then all that is connected to all the other souls, and to the main light that you know as GOD. What you should remember is that all souls together make GOD. You are part of this light. Never forget this.

52.

How do souls communicate with one another?

What do souls do?

Souls or spirits, or non-physical entities, do not need words to speak. They transfer emotions, knowledge and even lessons. There is no need to see, or touch one another, because the recollection of the wholeness of who each one is actually exists within all. To connect with each other, we summon with energy, and we speak with innate understanding. As all are connected with all there is no need for words, for conversation. We help one another with healing, with reminding them of lessons they have forgotten. This is why

reincarnations are important, to remind us of lessons learned, to help learn and not make the same mistakes. To expand with knowledge and understand what the other one faces because they have lived it once before.

Souls rest once they ascent right after a reincarnation. They built up the strength they lost while in physical, they review their lessons and paths of that life, to understand why it has taken the path it did. As one studies one's life, rests and rejuvenates, they can take upon yet another physical life, to gain more lessons, or they can relax, enjoy the natural emotion of unconditional love, pure joy that exists in spirit. One can also look after other souls to help them gain lessons. We are very fond of helping you see, we understand that we are all one and we do not hesitate to stop our own progression to help another proceed. One can also agree to reincarnate in the life of another just to help them learn valuable lessons, and pause their own journey.

But a spirit, also learns while in non-physical. Some do not choose to reincarnate to learn lessons, but choose to observe and study from experiences of others. Spirit guides also help as they share their own wisdom to less advanced souls, so they can gain more.

Spirits also "play". They rejoice with loved ones and linger in other non-physical worlds along with others. Being in spirit, still has skills that one needs to gain, they might choose to work on those.

There is no end to the things that one can do, you see, either in physical or non-physical there are always those who help, those who love you, those who oversee your progress, and the knowledge that you can learn, the expansion that you can take.

Do not think of other worlds and other dimensions while in this one, focus on the one you are and gain the best knowledge you can, be the happiest you can be, because this is the reason you are there.

53.

Is it possible for a body to have no soul? What is the purpose of the soul? When does the body end and the soul begin?

Soul brings meaning i.e. depth. The soul brings enlightenment, freedom, emotions. The soul guides the body to expansion, fulfillment. With no soul the body would be empty, strictly living to survive. Not realizing, not appreciating, not enjoying. It will be what you call "empty". Purpose brings meaning, and meaning brings happiness. Soul is responsible for that which you call happiness, joy and love. You are able to feel all those not because of your body, but because of your soul.

What would be the point of a body with no soul? It will be weak, with no purpose or meaning. All bodies have a soul, because soul completes it. It helps to document all the experiences, feelings and lessons and carries them on. Human bodies have a soul so that they experience and learn. Bodies with no soul will be in vain, with no purpose of existing. They will not exist because their death will be the end, their life will be with no meaning.

The one completes the other. Soul brings meaning, purpose and emotion while the body carries the soul so it learns and expands and experiences. Nothing exists without purpose, not now, not ever.

54.

How is the higher-self connected to our physical body? What is the purpose of this self and how does it interact?

Higher self is what you might call a soul. A soul has memory, it is a link to the past and the future, it guides, and it helps to fulfill a purpose. All of you have this connection, because otherwise you will be lost in the physical reality. You do not recall when the soul directs you, when it helps to flash your memory, when it shows you the way, but it does regularly. This is what we try to teach you, to listen to your inner voice, your soul that speaks and directs. It is connected to all you see, to all that was, and all that will be. But you have thoughts, and chatter and you get confused sometimes.

Re-direct yourself, stay in quiet, remove all those thoughts and you will gain insight, clarity. You will then see your pat as well as your purpose. Your connection with your higher self is clearer, and it helps you know, relax and move forward eagerly.

Higher self is not a different part of you, but an extension of you. It guides, leads, completes. This is you all of you, in combination with body and soul.

55.

Why are some people born on earth with kindness and love, while others with inner darkness? Why are there people who take pleasure in killing if we are all created equally?

There are people who are closer to their Divine nature. Those people envelope their light, they have clearer connection so they receive Divine healing and inspiration; they feel all those kind of emotions of the soul. Unfortunately, there are some other dear souls that block their Divine connection or deny it. As you block your Divine light, you embrace your physical aspect more. Alas the physical characteristics on their own are overpowered by greed, jealousy, and

144

ultimately darkness. As one is away from the light, they are closer to the darkness. When we say darkness we mean all emotions, thoughts and acts that you say are negative.

Think of it like the light brings pure emotions of joy, happiness, love and kindness. The further away you are from this connection, the more you embrace the opposite of those emotions. All of you are born with equal light, but you have your free will to choose which way to go. We do not impose such matters as to you. You can judge and experience and learn from your choices and mistakes.

If you embrace the light, you are given a fair share of pure emotions that go with it. If you observe and give kindness, then so it shall embrace you. The same is with love and joy, as you focus on those aspects, then light shine upon you. You do good deeds, not because you have to, but because light emanates from your heart and spreads towards others. You want to give to others, go ahead and help them. This is when light overflows to you and from you.

If you have no light to give, you spread misery to yourself and others. As one denies kind emotions, then what are they left with? Ultimately the sense of remorse fades. They take pleasure from the pain of

145

others, simply because they have pain inside. What you feel you spread to others. Those who kill do so with no remorse, with no shame because they do not feel kindness anymore, or love or appreciation. Their light has faded because they do not allow it to shine within them. Those will eventually return to the light, as all souls return to the light eventually. As they do, as light fills them once more, they will see the pain they caused; they will feel remorse. They will repent because they will see with the eyes of source. And once they do, they learn from their mistakes. They feel the pain they caused, their next lives will make different choices, and they will be different. Because you see, no one stays in the darkness for long. Not when there is so much light around.

56.

How are souls like Hitler treated in the afterlife?

Hitler was controlled by his need for victory, his need for power that conquered his inner and outer world. He had no friends, he didn't care for love, and he didn't feel the need to show any kindness. As he didn't feel those emotions, he didn't feel the need to give them either. He has grown up to become cold and relentless. He had choices nonetheless. He was not forced to take the actions that he did, he had his free will. Those actions made him who he was.

He had to face different pathways; he had more paths to choose from. Wars are not predestined, you see, they are not forced upon. They become options. The same way that many of the wars you do not know about has been avoided. Those paths were not picked by some people, they choose different paths. The road that Hitler chose has been chosen selfishly, egoistically, conquered by need for power. That need does not exist to one which is guided by light, but by one that is away from it. He was not created that way, he chose that way.

But as all return to the light eventually, so he did. His soul learns to cope with all that which he spread to others. He is still in isolation reviewing all those he had hurt, all those choices that he had to make and didn't. He too is learning from this process. When we say isolation we mean he has not yet reincarnated in another body, not will he do so soon. He has to learn from his past choices, understand them and see all those different paths he could have taken. As he relives them, he sees them clearly. Now his soul is in pain, now his light has returned, and he feels remorse, feels the pain. But we do not like to punish. He is there to understand, so he progresses, so he does not make the same mistakes, so he too can expand. But he has a long way to go still and we oversee his progress.

57.

Do fairies exist? What other supernatural beings exist?

Indeed, fairies are many of the wonderful souls that exist in non-physical dimensions. As we have mentioned before, there are many forms of life that exist, all meant to serve a purpose. Those "fairies" as you call them, exist as beams of light that move freely in one place to the other. They do not reside on earth, but they like to visit it a lot. Fairies, since they are energy, can easily move in one place to another, from one dimension to the next. Their purpose is not defined by their species. Each one has a different path to achieve, just the same way as you. They have many characters, similar to you and to us as none is the same as the other. This makes them experience in different ways, make different decisions.

A Fairy's path is sometimes to oversee an animal, help a flower grow, a flower to bloom, or even to help connect people with events, lost items or people. A fairy might choose to accompany a child in its play, or "punish" a person that mistreated a flower. Yes, fairies are protectors of nature, and they take it at heart if someone harms it in any way. They are "cheeky" spirits if we are to use this word in this way. They might make a fly drop in your milk, a leaf to stick under your shoe. We scold naughty fairies but they are quite capable of pulling tricks like this on anyone they dislike.

The fairies too help in the overall expansion. They pour energy on seeds so they grow. They like to call themselves "painters of nature". They also mend in people's lives, or get attached on a dear soul or most frequently to a child. As this happens, they help them in any way they can to brighten their days. Fairies help in the overall expansion by assisting the flow of order. They oversee animals, trees, and insects. In other planets they do this as well, but they mostly like to play and enjoy nature so they choose planets like earth. Their energy is smaller than the one of an angel, but they too are just as precious.

There are many other souls similar to the "fairies". They are the elves, as you might call them. They do not have a physical form but like to match colors and items. They have this unique transformational energy you see.

Elves exist in their own form; they are unique and have different qualities. They enjoy spending their time around animals. Elves are very shy creatures. They do not enjoy an interaction that is why they stay hidden from human eyes. They exist in spirit form, but they enjoy transforming and enjoying physical qualities as well. Elves are wiser than fairies. They take their task more seriously; they do not spend as much time playing. They are workers in their own way. They communicate with other spiritual beings and in some planets they felt comfortable enough to appear to other physical entities. Elves compose rhythm, music, they form the clouds, and they are also helpers to those in need. Some also work as mediators for higher beings. Their energy is loving, wise and you can interact with them only if they trust you enough. They are shy like this.

58.

Can we do magic? How does it work?

Magic is not for everyone. "The magic wand" exists within all. It is in the mind. But now everyone knows how to use it. Magic is all about bending the boundaries, doing things out of the ordinary realm. Magic is true, but it cannot be revealed but gradually be taught.

Anything that the mind can form, it can be created. Why does the mind form thoughts yet you cannot form them into reality? There is no reason as such. Through the years many people have mastered different techniques of what you might call "magic" or impossible. Yet they have disciplined themselves to achieve it. What the mind forms, it can be created. But the mind should not see it as impossible for it to occur.

There is no such thing as magic, but what it is in the real sense, is actually the power of the mind, the power of you. And it is not impossible; it is a matter of training your mind, and belief that it can happen. The more you work on something, the more you train your mind to belief it is true. The power that exists within you is equally the same as the one God applied when he formed so many things in the world. If God had said it was impossible then nothing of what exists today would have been here. For this, never say it is impossible. For us, nothing is magic because we know it can be done. For us it is only power, belief and discipline.

59.

*A*re spells real? *C*an one cast a spell with to help make things happen or dreams come true?

The word that you use to describe this does not resonate with us. The energy and assumption around this word and idea through the years is associated with lower energy. This is because the way that they have been used is filled with negative emotions and the people who seek them out choose materiality over spirit and put the ego before their actions. For this, we don't want to entrust you with tools that will make the ego side thrive in any way.

What is the purpose of "casting a spell" to make things happen? To dominate? To demand before God can give?

As you have understood, in no matter the way it is used, we are not fond of this act. Ask and you will receive, have faith, and pray for the highest good in mind. If what you ask is not indeed for your highest good, then it will not occur. Trust that whatever God decides, this is for the best and have faith in God's plan for you.

Many use this sort of 'spells" on others. Alas, you only bring bad things against yourselves.

Even if you use the forces of the universes to make things happen out the purest of your heart, even if you are not filled with ego and materiality, using uncalled forces to help you succeed in what you ask for, is not God's way.

Wicca or magic, or spells exerts universal forces to act for you. Those forces are not for your highest good, you seek out earthbound spirits and lower entities to help you work on a result. You may call for Divine light, yet that is not the way that it comes forward. What you receive is false light. And so, white or dark magic or spells, or Wicca, it is not associated with good forces nor the light.

If you want to have what you did not before, then pray to God to help you achieve that. Be appreciative and thankful of all that you do have and realize that if what you ask for is for your highest good then you shall receive it with the help of the true light.

That's all we give you about this topic.

60.

Do miracles happen? How and why?

The notion of "miracles" is not very clear to us. What is a "miracle" to you?

So if the notion of miracles to you is getting rescued from a physical death, or being shown the truth, or getting healed when you see no health, then the answer is yes. Miracles do occur. Usually they exist in the form of "hope" within everyone. This tiny bit of "hope" that a blind person has, wishing they can see again, it does not go in vain. As that bit of hope builds up, it creates momentum and it nudges one of us to assist. Whoever that is, what you call an Angel, or a Saint, or an ascended master, or a spirit guide, we know. With your hope you allow us to take action. Even if that is in a split second while an accident is occurring. If that person has the hope of being alive, then so we rush to "save" them.

For us it is nothing like a miracle. For us it is hope. For us, it is not just "we" saving you, but "you" having the desire to be saved. You save yourself.

And so, next time you think there is no saving, never lose your hope. There is always someone who is listening.

61.

What makes a saint? What happens to them once they return to non-physical?

What you call a saint or an ascended master is but a soul that has advanced well enough to expand their being. They become wiser, more purified. The pain is not the one that helps them advance, nor the sacrifice. It was their understanding of the truth. They stopped looking outside of themselves to be whole. They understood, accepted and advanced.

All of you will be ascended masters sooner or later. All of you advance and grow. Eventually, you won't need to learn any more, or grow, because you will be a perfect, version of yourself, complete.

Once one completes the lessons taken from a physical form, they continue to expand regardless reincarnations. Some of what you call "saints" have remerged to non-physical and help others teach, learn and expand. Others become emotions of love and unity, they become one with all, they re-emerge with what you call "god". They then do not differentiate from "God" but exist as one. This is the final process of a soul, it becomes truly complete aligned with the source of all that is.

62.

Is time travel even possible?

It is. We travel that way every second. This is how we are in many places at once. You do that as well while in spirit. In your physical reality time travel is not as easy however, you are on earth that has certain laws, like gravity and time. By using your physical body to time travel in any other time than the one you are in now is violating those laws. For this reason, it is not doable unless you train your spiritual gifts. What we mean is that your mind is not bound by space or time. Your mind does not go by "earth's laws". If you train your mind, you can indeed access different realities.

Nevertheless, remember that we are "spirit". We do not have a physical body. For this reason we do not carry any material body with us. To be able to time travel or astral project as some call it, you will need to be released from your physical body and this requires skill. But yes, you can time travel, you can visit any space you wish, however we do ask that you do it with caution and move wisely. We even argue against young spirit souls to travel around in realities and time. They can easily get lost you see. However, what we want to elaborate here is the fact that your spirit is just as powerful and not bound by restrictions.

62.

What should we do to find true peace?

We want to take a look upon animals. You find that they are at peace with all around, yes? They are in tune with their surroundings, with others, with their own body. Why is that? All of you, and then are born small, and then you grow older, you eat, live; you die from the physical body. So why are they at peace and you are not?

Looking at the differences between the two, there is reason, thought, ego. This is what differentiates you from them; this is what makes you lose your sense of true peace. So to be able to have peace, you have to find a way to balance thought and life. One to be able to work together with the other peacefully, there must be acceptance. Instead of judging, over thinking, and adding way to negative experiences and emotions try to subside them. Do not stress them but let them pass you by. Doing this, keeps you at peace, balanced with all that is around.

Think of it like a beautiful day in the sun. You are carefree, with your loved ones, you are happy. If a dark cloud comes up in the sky, do not let that ruin your day. Let the cloud float by and you will see the sun again. If you insist on putting your attention on that cloud, you will ruin your happy mood and your good day will come to an end. You see, in the same way your whole life is a sunny day. How many dark clouds are you going to allow to ruin your peace?

63.

Is it all fate or just coincidence?

No, not all things are predestined. Some are created by your thoughts and emotions. Others we sent on your path. That might be the people you encounter, the circumstances that comes your way, the thoughts that cross your mind. All events that occur however are a beautiful illustration of a perfectly balanced "map". When we say map, it is to help you picture it the way you know best; a map that connects with people, places and ideas. This "Map" constantly changes. It creates strings of connection between all those to help them get to an outcome, or a lesson.

Let's give you an example. Let's say one of your missions here on earth is to be able to share your knowledge with the less fortunate. A possible pathway for you would be to be able to teach in Africa. So the link that connects you to that place is possible. When it is time you are becoming aware of it. Some people that were "meant" to help you get there appear on your path to help you understand that path, to help you get on that path. However, from your experiences on earth, you form the desire of going on a journey to Egypt. This trip if completed will fill you with knowledge and give you an opportunity to make valuable connections. Your mother has a dream for you to be a doctor, and so she created a new route for you on the path, due to this desire. She created a path that leads you to Australia. Now all those paths are connected to you. All those paths have different outcomes. Those links on the "universal map" connect you with more countries, more people, and more events. Your attention and your choice however, is the one that defines the outcome. All those are created and connected. We might even send you people to help you get to Africa or Australia. But do you speak to them? Do you want their help? Perhaps you ignore them and off to Egypt you go. And so, with this we want to help you understand that most events, people or circumstances are in fact linked to you, but not to one end result. You are the one that defines the end result.

64.

Why are some people born intuitive and others not?

All are born intuitive. Some however, choose to "shut down" this gift by ignoring it. Others trust it, and thus they enhance it. As that comes clearer, so their intuition increases. Intuition helps you connect with spirit. If you trust the responses from the universe, you believe in the truth of the spirit that speaks to you.

Many occurrences cause a child to ignore their gift. For some it might be fear, others rely more on their environment and learn to trust the ego more than their true nature. It is natural for a child to have increased intuition and speak to spirit, but for an adult it takes practice and determination. This is so, not because some are born with it and some not, but because some trust it, believe and accept it, while others not.

Intuition is relying on your own instincts. Thought is the opposite of intuition. Silence the one for the other to thrive. All of you have this gift innate, learn to explore it and it shall become evident within you.

65.

Wholeness. How do we become whole?

Wholeness comes as you become one with all that is. That includes your mind, soul and body, nature, other beings and even spirits. As you connect with all there is, you become complete. For spirit it is easier to be whole because they are connected with all already. You, as incarnations in human form, go by the ego that differentiates you with everyone and everything. As you silence the ego, you connect with all that is. This is where your true power lies.

66.

What is the false light and why do they intervene when we ask to speak to Angels or Jesus?

"The false light". What the term signifies does not exist. There is only one true light. Anything less than that is not called light, nor is a true representation of Holy Spirit.

We ask that you are not fearful of it, as it cannot harm if you don't allow it. There are spirits who have lost their way, their fearful of the consequences of their actions so they hide and run from the light. Some have been removed from their true light so that they heal, see their actions and learn from them. Some have denied such a request and so they have denied their responsibilities and their divinity. They are too fearful to return to the light and so they might disguise as

Divine beings. Some want to confuse you, make you lose your way the same way they have lost their own. Others just exist and belong where you are and they intervene with no purpose. They enjoy human connection and they find pleasure in being called forward in a connection with you. You can easily cast those away with prayer.

Others feed on sadness and angst. They enjoy those emotions as they create negative energy. Those are the lower spirits who want to create fear and pain. We guard you when you pray so those cannot come close to you.

And so, when you ask us why these beings come forward. We tell you that they too, are free of their choices. They don't resonate with the one of God, of the true light, the same as some people in the physical world mistreat and cause pain. Both exist in the physical and in spirit. How do you handle those people while in human form? You stay away from them; you allow them to reap what they have sowed. Similarly those darker energies will not be for long. There are a group of deities that watches out for those spirits. Their choices do not go unnoticed.

Have faith in the light, only pray to the light and ask that true guidance comes through to help you. The more you fear and turn your attention to those, you seek them out. If you feel you are in their presence cast them away at once.

171

When you are in the presence of the true light, you feel the inner peace, the love. The answers flow to you freely, with no resistance. When the light speaks, there are no interferences. Allow our words to move freely between your fingertips as you type our responses. You are in our presence, the presence of the true light of God. Allow those other beings to exist, the same as you exist freely, and the same that you have your choices and free will, they have their own. It might not be in resonance with God's plan for them, but they too learn. They shall return to the light as the only thing that exists is the light.

If you feel threatened, by those who have digressed away from the light, then embrace the light some more. They have no purpose bothering any one that is surrounded by the light that is connected to God. They only want to interact with those who are in doubt, fear and further from God and the light. Be wary of those shadowy spirits, and stay close to the light. If you wish to connect with lighted beings, pray. It is the strongest form of protection that we can give you. Then you shall be safe.

67.

Is it wrong to channel the Angels or ask them directly questions that trouble us?

Why would it be wrong to connect with lighted beings that are created to restore order and help those in need? Does this sound like something that God instructed for you?

If you call for an angel, will God be upset with you? Will He deny you? Angels are true representation of God or source or light. Whatever they speak comes directly from God. Speaking or connecting or praying to one or the other is the same as it is a representation of the true light of God.

Consider this. If a student speaks to the teacher about a problem, will the headmaster be angry? If a child asks his brother and not his parent about a matter of

173

concern, will they be upset? What if a woman speaks to a nun and not to a priest about guidance, does the advice of the nun considered less valid? Does the word of the teacher, or the brother?

No. as long as guidance comes from a place of love and understanding it shall be good guidance. Similarly, the Angels or any other form of lighted being can connect with you if you ask them for help. If God does not allow any sort of interaction other than the one with source itself, then why do the angels exist? Why does any sort of light respond to you and guides you?

Does it sound true to you to call for the light and the light not to respond to your angst? Does it seem like something that God would have instructed? If your prayers to the light, to any light, angel or saints are not responded to, and instead only lower beings can connect with you?

If that will be so there will be a disorder. If only lower beings connected with humans when they prayed and asked for guidance, then only false guidance would exist. Where does the light stand?

And so, what you have heard is wrong. God wants you to connect with the light, with any form of light God, or source, angel or saints or spirit guides as long as they are connected to the light, the guidance will be true and pure. Do not hesitate to speak to God or an angel of the lord and guidance will come through to reach you, anytime and anywhere.

68.

Is using divination tools, wrong? How should we use divination tools the right way so that they are acceptable by you?

If divination tools as you call them, are used to predict the future or to force guidance to appear, or asked to make choices for you, then in any way and form they are used, it is wrong.

We are aware that so many of you use divination tools with a pure heart, not meant to spread harm or act unjustly. Even those you call angel cards or those means that you pray to holy spirits to respond through, if done so to force those mentioned above, then the guidance that you seek will not come through. It is not because we don't want to help you but there are some answers that we cannot give you. Firstly questions about the future are unpredictable. As future changes, as you change, so do your choices and your future. We cannot respond to you if you ask us what will happen, simply because it is not predestined.

What's more is asking us what to do. Deciding for you is not the way that God instructs. We can help you shed some light in one way or the other, or guide you to find the right path, but we cannot make any decision for you or force you to change your mind. For this, we are very careful when helping you about such matters. When you ask us for guidance and the cards interpretation are fixed and they give you "yes do this" or "no don't act" then if we give you one or the other card we are forcing the decisions.

Another matter that is hard to define through divination tools is giving you clear guidance. Yes we can help you through angel cards, or pendulum drawing or any other tool but the guidance is very restricted. If you don't use your intuition to receive direct messages then the interpretation and guidance is vague and can be easily misinterpreted.

Many times the words we want to say to you don't belong in cards and are not a yes/ no sort of answer. Instead of giving you false guidance, we don't respond. Many times your questions are full of ego and you force one answer to come through and denying anything other than that. The ego makes you see what you want. "Yes you will get a lot of money", "yes you will meet your true partner", "no you don't need to act". Many of the answers are ego based and not angel inspired. For this you should be very careful when using any sort of divination tools as the answers might not be from source.

Also, using any sort of divination without prayer, is inventing any sort of energies to mend with your tools and guide them. In this case, the answers can be false and not true. For this, we want you to be aware of the loopholes inherent in them.

With all of these in mind, we return to your question. Are divination tools wrong? The answer is no. they are only tools. The person who uses them should be open to the truth and invite Divine guidance through them. Not restrict nor force that guidance to come through. When you use any sort of divination, don't be restricted, and listen, we might speak to you directly, and not through the tools.

Are you aware of our guidance?

Pay attention.

69.

How can I make the right choices?

In this physical life in which you now are, you have made choices. The choices you make don't define who you are, but define who you become. With every choice you make, you create a new aspect of your life. This choice has lessons or coincidences to you and to those around. This does not mean however that you should dread making a mistake. Mistakes don't exist, only different lessons. You gain something good with each decision that you make.

We don't want you to be afraid of making choices. In any direction that you go, you gain. Sometimes the lessons come harder than others, but in all cases they help you to grow.

Many of you ask "how to make the right choice?" "How do I know which decision will be best for me?" this is the reason of my visit here now, to help you understand the process behind the decision making, so you do not dread another important life decision.

As this important decision comes to your path, you cannot know what each choice will bring you. What you can do however is consider what you want that outcome to be. What do you want to gain out of each choice? How do you want it to affect you? As you decide what that, you decide the outcome. With some reflection, and pause you will soon gain the clarity that you need for the "right decision". What is the Right decision for you, since you have already decided the outcome that you wish to receive?

Let us give you a defining example. You get offered multiple job offerings. They are different job positions, different places, and different experiences. At this point you should reflect upon what you want the outcome to be. How do you see yourself feeling after a year of work there? Do you see yourself thriving at that job, gaining great experience and credentials? Do you see yourself getting a promotion and climbing up the ladder to a better position soon? Or perhaps you envision a warm welcoming environment with friendly co-workers and relaxing time schedule? Perhaps you even wish to have more salary in the years to come? Each of these desires, result to a different outcome. In the beginning you don't know what you want, so the right choice for you is not clear. As you decide and reflect, then the right position will become clear to you. All you have to do know, is sit back, clear your mind, give it some time and you will have great clarity and a "knowing" as to which position will be right for you.

This is the way the universe works, and this is the way "we" help you to make the "right choices" for you.

What's more, you are fearful of those life paths that give you "hard lessons". Alas sometimes, you cannot create a beautiful building without some work. Don't dread of the hard-coming lessons, instead trust that those too, have an important lesson to bring you, to make you a greater person. We want to remind you that some of those "hard-lessons" were put in your path from your own higher self, to mold you into an even more exceptional being.

At this time, we want to salute you, and hope that our words will make you stand greater with no fear, and no procrastination, because the choices you make, define your future.

70.

What does the buzzing in one ear mean?

When this occurs, more often than not, you receive Divine information through the subconscious. This is to help you with a problem or give you ideas to move forward. Your higher-self connects with you this way, but your conscious is not aware. Allow the process to take place with no fear and worry. It is a blessed time to heal and recover.

Divine healing and guidance occurs very often in your life, when you mostly need it. Those who are more sensitive to energies feel it or sense it, and others hear this buzzing in the ears. For those who see this process take place, they will see colors of light coming through the connection cord.

You also receive this sort of input while sleeping.

71.

Does Feng Shui work?

"Certain elements hold purer energy than others; they affect your own energy. This is true for all objects new and old pretty, and ugly.

This is how it comes about. Objects as anything else absorbs energy from others. The positive or negative attention they receive whenever someone observes them makes a particular object absorb that energy and then emits it accordingly to the people that are in their environment. Imagine how you would feel getting into an old, unclean space with ugly objects and entering a new furnished and well decorated room with beautiful colors. This is energy that you observe and emit.

Yes, Feng shui does work and it has to do with how it affects your energy and concentration. A messy desk for instance causes you to lose things, have a pile of papers and things to do so it offers disorientation and overwhelms you. Additionally, certain colors provide peace while others extra energy. Certain symbols, elements and objects have more empowerment or introduce a variety of different benefits. There are some that are used for financial growth while others for health and so on. The art of feng shui in fact provides many advantages to those who are ready for a change. Be aware however, that too much information is added and altered as time progresses and there's no need to go by every detail according to feng shui experts. In other words you don't have to do anything that you read in a book, as that would be unnecessary and stressful for you. Make changes in your home while trusting your intuition and it will guide you to the changes needed to make.

Relax, clear your mind and ask us to show you what changes to make in each room. Let the thoughts then be created and trust your third eye vision. What we suggest to all for now is to clear your space from clutter and old objects. Remember don't keep anything that you do not like, instead replace it or transform it to something you enjoy looking at.

72.

*W*hy don't we remember our past lives? *I*s there something that we do remember or something we can do to remember?

As you agree to join a new lifetime, you agree to embrace all the qualities and characteristics of that new person you are becoming. This is to receive the lessons with ease and to make choices according to what you have learned and believe. If all the lives you had lived before were entwined in one self, then all those lessons, experiences and choices would be affected by them.

If you were fearful of the darkness in one life, then this means that all the lives would continue on that effect enabling you to fight your fears and affecting your life choices. The same goes with everything that you have faced in each lifetime. The reason that you don't remember it is in fact a gift. Ignorance is a protective shield against fears, insecurities and drama. Some of the paths that you face now, might be a bridge to help you face one or two of the past fears that kept you grounded. For this, you might find yourself remembering or sensing parts of past lives, to help you work through them and release them. However all of them together will only weaken your current life.

Enjoy the gift of ignorance and trust that all works according to God's Divine plan for you.

73.

*W*hy do some children remember their past life when they are young?

It is true, this sort of occurrence happens. The feelings that come from intuition are very strong. These children have heightened intuition as it will help them on their path in that lifetime. The effects of having advanced intuition, is memory that comes from source, from their higher self. That sort of memory cannot be denied nor controlled. For a pure mind such as the one of a child, when memories of the higher self, become evident, they are not denied, nor questioned, nor hidden and so they become realized with no difficulty by the child.

Why do you think you don't often have those sorts of memories? The truth is you do, but your ego is more advanced and your fears grow stronger so you question that intuition, that memory that you don't understand. Many times that memory comes from dreams, or through feelings you cannot explain. You too have heightened intuition but you do not allow it to dominate.

The question is not why those children have these sorts of memories, but why don't you?

74.

Are the alternative forms of medicine accepted by God and the angels? How does reiki or Pranic healing work according to your guidance?

It is a way that God intended for energy to radiate, and reform, and recharge, and heal. What you are is energy, the way your cells work and interact have their own energy. To be able to connect with that energy to heal, it is a gift that God provided openly to help you explore and recover. By connecting with energy in that way, you are fulfilling God's intention that energy should be used and formulate and give life.

To respond to your question briefly, it is acceptable and it is a Godly gift to heal through the power of universal energy. Explore it, learn it, use it and teach it forward, but remember this: always do it with the purest heart. Energy is light, and it is pure. The hands that handle it should be so as well before they direct it to another. Also, as you use this Divine gift of "energetic" healing, remember to do it with the purest emotions. The ones that receive such a healing are open and grateful for it to fulfill its purpose.

We, angels use it also to help those who ask for help. "Prana" as some call it is the energy of God that heals.

75.

How do I forgive and move forward with my life without looking in the past?

Pain is temporary, it is not meant to stay. Whatever you have experienced in your life, it should not keep you from the rest of your life. What God wants for you is not yet fulfilled, your path here on earth is still blooming, as you are asking us this question about how to move forward, we are certain that you are not far off your true path.

Whatever brought you here, in this book, in this current question, is a sign of growth and improvement. We tell you this now and please hear us with an open heart: "you can now leave the past be, and carry on stronger. We know that the past has changed you; we also know that it was made you who you are now. And who you are now, we wouldn't change for nothing else. Because right now, you are perfect and we want you to see yourself in this way as well.

Holding in pain for yourself and others, it is only keeping the past's wounds open. To let them heal, you must forgive. To forgive another or even yourself, you have to make amends with whoever you are now, with whatever has happened in the past. Don't forget that the past cannot be changed, but your attitude towards them can. And if you are able to stand here now and ask us this, then you are ready to forgive and carry on.

If you are full of anger for another, we tell you this now: let God be a judge for their actions. If they have harmed you, then they will have to know of your pain. God will show them in one way or another and make them understand what their choices and actions have brought. This is not to be punished, but to learn. This is the way that they can thrive.

And so, you will be able to thrive if you carry on forward. If you did wrong another, recognize the pain that you put them in. If you have done one wrong, then do three times another good to another. Ask for repentance but first forgive yourself. If you do then God shall forgive you and God doesn't judge your choices. God and we know what the truth is in you now. You are ready to carry on with a lighter heart. So speak to yourself, and tell it that you forgive them.

76.

How can I be more giving and less guided by ego?

Find the peace inside of yourself. As you find peace then you will know that you are perfect with what you have now. If you can spare that of which you have, will you share it now?

Will a battle between your ego and your inner voice begin? This means you don't give with a full heart. To change that, we want you to pray; as you pray before you give that of which you have, you make the exchange purer. Don't expect anything in return. If you give to have something else, then this won't succeed. Give only so that the others can have more.

Don't differentiate others from you, as what they have now; you might have more in other times and in another way. So what if they have a bigger house, you have a bigger family, or more friends. Don't think that what another has is more than you and be jealous. You all share God's gifts equally. What you own they might have later and what they have that you need, it shall come if you are grateful of all that exist in your life. God makes no mistakes. Appreciate what you have, say thank you for all you have, for all you appreciate, recognize them often. And thus, you won't be jealous of others anymore. Then you won't hesitate to give to another because you know that you have so many already.

If you can't share your belongings with another, it is because you don't recognize how many you have already. Didn't you know that once you appreciate what you have, you will never run out of resources? Tell that to yourself often, and tell that to others. Say "thank you" for having more and it is okay to give to others.

FIND MORE AMELIA BERT'S BOOKS:

1.   2.   3.

1. <u>NUMBER SEQUENCES AND THEIR MESSAGES-</u> Do you get a glimpse of repetitive numbers? Do you notice number sequences like 1111, 222, 44 often? They are not random, they bring you messages. They are Angel Numbers and in this booklet, you will learn all about them. Unravel them; discover their Divine Guidance.

2. **<u>THE BOOK OF DIVINE MESSAGES</u>** - This book shares 365 divinely guided messages for daily assistance or instant support. <u>Instructions of use:</u> Clear your mind and ask what you want you need assistance with. Flip through

the pages of the book and you will be guided to stop to the right message for you at that time.

3. THE GUIDEBOOK TO YOUR INNER POWER: This book presents spiritual practices in a step by step process to help you unleash your inner potential. Discover explanations, techniques and secrets in a broad how-to guide for all.

4.   5.   6.

4. **THE TRUTH OF ALL THAT IS -** This spiritual book, links all the peaces together, by revealing the truth of the cosmos. Find the light and presence of the Angels beautifying your life as you right along their words. *An*

amazon best seller. *(Also available in Spanish: "La verdad te todo lo que es").*

5. **COLORING TO LIFE: DESIRES AND EMOTIONS -** This is not your usual coloring book; it provides you with 28 unique coloring sketches that present ultimate wishes and desirable emotions. As you color them, you invite their frequency to merge with your own, and ultimately manifest them into your life.

6. **COLORING TO LIFE: ARCHANGES AND ASCENTED MASTERS** - This is not your usual coloring book; it is infused with spiritual power from 27 Archangels & Ascended Masters. As you color, these lighted entities surround you, sharing their energy with you for instant healing, guidance and spiritual power.

GET Another of Amelia Bert's eBooks for FREE!

HERE IS HOW:

If you enjoyed this book, please do give a good review on the website you have purchased the book from.

1. Leave your review on the bookstore you have purchased this book from.

2. Send a screenshot picture of the review on: Amelia@ameliabert.com including the ebook that you are interested in acquiring.

3. You will receive the eBook in your email within 72 hours.

About the Author:

Amelia Bert is a freelance author and online journalist. At twenty five, she discovered her intuitive side, and mastered the clairaudient and clairvoyant ability to connect with spirit. She chooses to solely communicate with lighted spirits such as Angels that guide and inspire her.

She works closely with the Angels, through her psychic abilities. She gathers wisdom and information in that way, and shares it through her books and meditations. She aims to help others make a connection with their higher consciousness and discover their life's purpose.

Amelia has a degree in English language and literature. She spends her time writing, learning from the Angels, and painting. She lives with her husband and two cats and she plans to travel the world.

Find out more, visit: https://ameliabert.com

GET ASSISTANCE FROM THE ANGELS

Do you want to connect with Amelia and the Angels to get direct assistance on your path, and answers to your questions?

Amelia is currently offering intuitive readings with your Guardian Angels and Spirit Guides. All you have to do is reach out.

We help you with an exclusive one time discount of 20% for any intuitive readings in the website:

http://bit.ly/1LGvTTT

Your answers are only a few clicks away.

86365505R00115

Made in the USA
San Bernardino, CA
28 August 2018